SOME BITS OF HISTO.

Legendary site of the boar's well   J C Senior

LOCAL HISTORY TALKS GIVEN AT GLYDE HOUSE, BRADFORD

BY

JANET C SENIOR

2018

All illustrations in the book are acknowledged. Photographs attributed to J C Senior are not for general use. The postcards used contain no publisher or photographer information. Many thanks to Mary Tetlow for providing extra illustrations. Cover photograph is a waterfall in the Botanical Garden at Lister Park.

Published by

The Bradford Historical and Antiquarian Society

ISBN 978-1-9996419-0-0

CONTENTS

ACKNOWLEDGEMENTS

Without the help and advice of the staff at West Yorkshire Archive Service Bradford and the Local History Library Bradford these talks would not have been possible. Many thanks to you all, especially for your patience and interest. Thanks, are also due to the owners and staff at Glyde House for providing such a marvellous venue and letting me invade them every month.

Thanks also to Bob Duckett, Bradford Historical and Antiquarian Society, for ploughing through my thoughts and supporting this enterprise.

Finally, my thanks to the Bradford Historical and Antiquarian Society for financing the publication.

Note. Throughout the book the initials WYAS stand for West Yorkshire Archive Service and the initials BLSL stand for Bradford Local Studies Library.

INTRODUCTION

After attending Bolling Girls' Grammar School in Bradford, I went to Neville's Cross Teacher Training College in Durham where I qualified as a teacher in 1965. At college, I studied Ancient History and Archaeology, interests that have remained with me all my adult life. After taking early retirement from working as a special school teacher in Bradford, I was employed as an assistant librarian at the Yorkshire Archaeological Society in Leeds. Amateur archaeology remained part of my life and I went on as many excavations as I could until arthritis hampered my ability to kneel. Since then I have written or co-written four history books and given numerous talks throughout Yorkshire.

In late 2014, a friend invited me to meet for a coffee at Glyde House after realising I had never been there. I remembered the building from my childhood as being part of the Children's Department of the Bradford Council. To my astonishment, it now had offices for the Labour Party, was a music and meeting venue and ran a very pleasant café. My friend introduced me to the owners and the general manager as a "local historian". Immediately I was shown a magnificent Bradford Coat of Arms and questioned closely on the items represented. Before I knew it, I had agreed to give a talk at Glyde House on the story of the Bradford Coat of Arms. Since that date, I have given numerous talks on different aspects of Bradford's history from Anglo Saxon times to the present day. The choice of topics usually follows research at the West Yorkshire Archive Service Bradford or a chance remark by one of the visitors. The talks are given on the first Monday of each month and it has become quite a social gathering. I call my talks "taster talks". The aim is, that after my introduction to the subject, the listeners will be encouraged to undertake further research on their own. This book is a compilation of nine of these talks.

J C Senior

September 2017

CHAPTER ONE

THE LEGEND OF THE BOAR OF BRADFORD

This was the first talk I gave at Glyde House. The owners had purchased a stone carving of the Bradford Coat of Arms from the old police station in Wakefield Road. At our first meeting, they were under the impression that the brick object on the chevron indicated Bradford had a castle in the middle ages. After pointing out their misunderstanding I was asked to give a talk on the subject.

Until 1976 the Bradford Coat of Arms was a pictorial representation of the legend of the Boar of Bradford.

The original Bradford Coat of Arms on an old tram at the Bradford Industrial Museum

J C Senior

The main components of the story are depicted: a boar's head without a tongue, an oak tree to represent a wood, a well to represent a spring, and three horns. Whether the story is true or not is debatable, but it has been believed by citizens of Bradford for many centuries. Some aspects of the legend are based on facts and other aspects which, though not provable, are quite believable.

The legend dates to the time of John of Gaunt, Duke of Lancaster. After the Norman Conquest Bradford was part of the holdings of Ilbert de Lacy. De Lacy came to England with William the Conqueror and was given lands throughout the kingdom as a reward for his support. Large sections of Yorkshire became de Lacy holdings. Bradford remained in de Lacy hands until the late 14th century. Henry de Lacy, 3rd Earl of Lincoln and Baron of Pontefract, died in 1311 with no male heir. His only daughter Alice de Lacy became his heir and, because of her wealth, the King, Edward I, arranged for her to marry his nephew Thomas of Lancaster, heir to the Earldom of Lancaster. The marriage settlement gave Thomas control of all Alice's lands during his lifetime. Thomas was captured at Boroughbridge after he rebelled against the king and was executed at Pontefract Castle.

Alice should have regained control of the de Lacy holdings, but the king imprisoned her until she agreed to sign away her rights. On her death, the de Lacy lands in Yorkshire passed to her nephew by marriage, Henry 1st Duke of Lancaster. John of Gaunt married the 1st Duke's eldest daughter, Blanche of Lancaster. When the 1st Duke died in 1361 John received half his lands and the title Earl of Lancaster. **Blanche's sister died in**

1362. John now inherited all the Lancaster possessions and his father, King Edward III, made him Duke of Lancaster. John spent a great deal of his time in the North of England travelling between his various properties. The route from his castle in Pontefract to his castle in Lancaster took him through Bradford Dale.

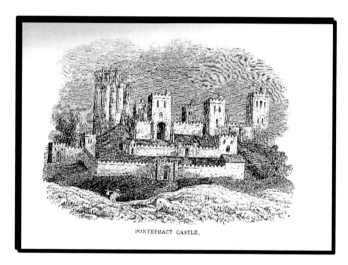

From Chronicles of Old Pontefract by Lorenzo Padgett

Bradford Dale contained several manors, which are now part of the City of Bradford. The manors of Bolton, Eccleshill, Bowling, Magna Horton, Horton, Clayton, Thornton, Allerton, **Heaton** and Manningham surrounded the small town of Bradford. Inhabitants of these manors would travel to Bradford for church services and to trade in its markets. The church in Bradford was the only one in the area and markets were often held in its churchyard. Streams flowed down the hillsides to join the Bradford Beck which provided a power source, water and fish for the town. Most of the hillsides were covered with trees. The parish church was known as the "Church in the Wood". Cliffe Wood stretched to the north of the church along the banks of the Beck towards the River Aire.

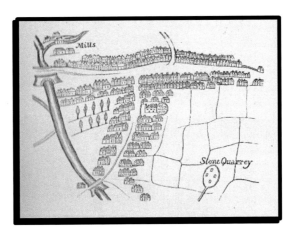

From The History and Topography of Bradford by John James

The layout of the town's streets can still be seen today. Kirkgate, starting near the church, passed over Church Bridge and continued westward to meet Westgate from the north and Ivegate from the south. Where they met became the Market Place for the town and here stood the market cross, the toll booth and the town lockup. On each side of the streets were crofts with tofts behind them. The town was beginning to expand and was quite a busy place.

Contrary to some beliefs there was never any castle in Bradford. There was a manor house but no physical evidence has been found of such a building dating to this period. An Inquisition of the Duke of Lancaster's holdings was undertaken in 1311. It stated,

The Earl hath at Bradford an Aulum (Hall) with chambers

It goes on to say that it needed repairing. As the Lord of the Manor was technically the Duke of Lancaster the Hall was his, but he rarely dwelt there. Each of the surrounding manors also had manor houses which were inhabited by the Lords of those manors.

So, the scene is set.

At that time, many areas of the country were infested with wild boars. These wild boars were a danger to the inhabitants and many people were killed by them. A male wild boar can weigh up to 200kg (440pounds).

One such boar was inhabiting Cliffe Wood and causing problems for any person travelling by foot from Manningham to Bradford. Legend says that the Lord of the Manor offered a reward to anyone who could kill the boar. The story does not state which Lord of the Manor this was. It may have John of Gaunt himself on one of his visits to the town or maybe his representative.

An inhabitant of the Manningham area of Bradford, thought to be a member of the Northrop family, was walking through Cliffe Wood near the Parish Church when he saw the boar drinking from a well. Northrop was armed and managed to

Cliffe Wood area on Canal Road Bradford   J C Senior

spear the boar killing it instantly. He now had a dilemma. He had been on an errand and could not go directly to claim the reward. So, Northrop cut out the tongue, placed it in his pouch, retrieved his spear and went on his way. Not long afterwards another man came along and saw the dead boar. He did not notice the tongue was missing and decided to claim the reward. The boar was far too heavy for him to carry so he cut off its head and made his way to where the reward was to be presented. This man was greeted as a hero and the reward was just about to be presented when Northrop appeared. He produced the tongue thus proving he had killed the boar and claimed his reward.

Postcard of the killing of the boar. Personal collection of J C Senior

James Hartley, a Bradford schoolmaster, wrote that the reward was a piece of land in Horton Magna known by the name of Hunt Yard. Also, every year on St Martin's Day, 11th November, Northrop or his heirs were to go to the Market Place in Bradford with a hunting dog and blow his horn three times. Richard Gough' in his publication of William Camden's "Britannia" published in 1789, said that John of Gaunt granted to John Northrop of Manningham and his heirs three messuages and six bovates of land in Horton. Northrop had to attend John of Gaunt and his heirs yearly in winter when the Duke was travelling between his possessions. **He was to wait upon the Duke for thirty days with a lance and a hunting dog and for this he would be paid 1d and ½d for his** dog. Northrop was employed to ensure the safe passage of the Duke through his lands in this area. In later years one Northrop granted some of the land to Rushworth of Horton so that Rushworth could hold the lance and hound whilst Northrop blew his horn. These were the words spoken

Heirs of Rushworth come hold me my hound while I blow three blasts with my horn, to pay the rent due to our sovereign Lord King.

Gough says that the tradition of the blowing of the horn was still being followed in 1789 with the original horn. Note that the rent is now due to the king. Lancaster's lands became crown lands when Henry Bolingbroke, son of John of Gaunt, became King Henry IV in 1399.

The horn blowing ceremony drawing by Mary Tetlow

The Northrops were a prominent family who lived in the Manningham area of the city until well into the 19th century. In the 1379 Poll Tax Johannes de Northrop & Ux paid iiijd. At the 1612 Inquisition William Northrop was a juror for Manningham. During the 18th century one of the Ushers at the

Boys Grammar School was Thomas Northrop. There is a monument to a William Northrop, who died in 1800, in Bradford Cathedral. His lands included nearly all Girlington, Cliffe Fields opposite the entrance to Manningham Lodge, the site of Whetley Reservoir, land in Lumb Lane, houses in Church Street and Globe Mill in Brick Lane End. When William died, a relation Thomas Northrop managed the lands for William's widow. During the 19th century members of the family moved to Heaton, Great Horton and Clayton. There are descendants of the family still living in the city, but the tradition of Blowing the Horn is no longer carried out.

Plaque in Hunt Yard Great Horton   J C Senior

GLOSSARY

Croft – the name for the dwelling of peasants

Toft – the land around a croft where peasants kept animals and raised a few vegetables.

Messuage – house with surrounding land and outbuildings

Bovate – as much land as an ox could plough in a year

Ux or Uxor- wife

Poll Tax – everyone over the age of 14 had to pay a groat (4d.) to the Crown.

Inquisition – trials for heresy by both Catholic and Protestant churches. The last one took place in England in 1612. Condemned were burnt.

Usher – an assistant teacher in the grammar school probably not a university graduate who taught non-classical subjects.

REFERENCES

William Cudworth	Rambles Round Horton	1886
Joseph Fieldhouse	Bradford	1972
Horace Hird	Bradford in History	1968
John James	The History and Topography of Bradford	1841
Margaret Law	The Story of Bradford	1912
William Scruton	Pen and Pencil Pictures of Old Bradford	1889

CHAPTER TWO

THE ESTABLISHED CHURCH IN BRADFORD FROM THE SEVENTH TO THE SEVENTEENTH CENTURY.

I have long been interested in the early history of the town of Bradford. This period cannot be studied without looking at the development of religious establishments in the area. The management of the established church before and after the reforms of Henry VIII gives an insight to life in the town over a period of nearly a thousand years.

Saint Paulinus brought Christianity to the West Riding of Yorkshire in the seventh century. He was sent to England by Pope Gregory in 601 to work with Saint Augustine. Edwin, the King of Deira (the part of Northumbria which included what is now Yorkshire) married Aethelburh, sister of the King of Kent. Her chaplain, Paulinus, travelled with her to Deira so she could practice Christianity in a pagan area. He was consecrated Bishop Paulinus before he left the south of England. King Edwin and his nobles were converted to Christianity. He probably founded the church at Dewsbury where there is an ancient stone which reads

Hic Paulinus praedicavit et celebravit

Here Paulinus preached and celebrated.

This is recorded in Bede's *Ecclesiastical History of the English People* along with this reference

In Campodonum where there was a royal dwelling he built a church.

Dewsbury Minster, as the church became known, was the mother church for an area of over 400 square miles stretching from Wakefield in Yorkshire to Burnley in Lancashire. Daughter churches would provide wealth for the minster through the payment of tithes.

Bradford, at this time, was a remote area. It had a few dwellings near the waterway which ran through steeply wooded valleys. It grew up around the safest crossing point over the waterway where there was a ford. Bradford supposedly takes its name from this ford – Broad Ford. The area fell within the remit of the minster at Dewsbury and eventually missionaries were sent to the area to covert the inhabitants to Christianity. The missionaries were successful and established a church on the hillside above the waterway which became known as the church in the wood. They were not as successful in Eccleshill where the missionaries were supposedly stoned by the inhabitants.

The "Church in the Wood" was built of wood and stood for many years on the spot where the present Cathedral stands. The only physical evidence for this church are the remains of Saxon Crosses which can be found in the present church fabric. This church was in a poor condition when the Normans conquered the area in 1066. William the Conqueror rewarded his Norman supporters by dividing England into estates which he doled out to them. Much of present day Yorkshire was given to Ilbert de Lacy. Ilbert and Walter de Lacy were the sons of Hugh de Lacy of Lassy in the Calvados department of Normandy France. They travelled to England with Duke William hoping for rich rewards.

The de Lacy Knot from "The Coats of Arms of the Nobility and Gentry of Yorkshire" by J Horsfall Turner

After the Conquest Walter received lands in Hertfordshire and Shropshire whilst Ilbert's rewards were parts of Lancashire (including the Forest of Bowland), Lincolnshire, Nottinghamshire and West Yorkshire. Ilbert took part in the Harrying of the North. One of his first actions when peace was restored was to build a secure base in the area. Pontefract Castle was constructed c1070 and Ilbert was then created Baron of Pontefract. His holdings in Yorkshire became known as the Honor of Pontefract. Bradford was now part of the Honor of Pontefract.

As the Lord of the manor Ilbert also held the patronage of the church in Bradford. The church being in sad repair needed replacing. The Lacy's paid for a new church to be constructed, this time in stone, and it lasted for nearly 300 years. The early years of the 14th century saw bands of Scotsmen raiding the North of England. It is believed that one of these bands caused **the destruction of the first stone church in 1327. The Honor of** Pontefract was now in the hands of Alice de Lacy who had - 15married Thomas Earl of Lancaster. She died in 1348 and her possessions went to her nephew Henry who was created the 1st Duke of Lancaster by King Edward III. The estates of the Dukes of Lancaster passed through marriage to John of Gaunt in 1362. John of Gaunt was a son of Edward III and his son was Henry Bolingbroke. Henry was exiled to France by Richard II and barred from becoming Duke of Lancaster. On Gaunt's death in 1399 Henry returned to England primarily to reclaim the Lancaster holdings. However, he ousted Richard from the throne and became King Henry IV. He added the Lancastrian lands to the Crown possessions. So, Bradford became part of the Crown lands. This meant that the patronage of the church was now in royal hands and it remained so until the 17th century.

Postcard of Bradford Parish Church from author's private collection.

Bradford vicars/rectors were at times colourful characters. In 1335 Henry de Latrynton was accused of appropriating manorial lands. He was found guilty and fined. He did not lose his post. He had been felling wood. Someone had reported him removing three cartloads of wood including an entire oak tree from the manorial park. William Rhodes died in 1401 a very rich man. In his will, he asked for his body to be buried in the chancel of the church. The recipients of his wealth were

William the chief parish clerk	12d.
William Northrop minor parish clerk	12d.
The mother church of St Peter, York	6s. 8d.
The Friars at Holy Trinity, Knaresborough	40d.
The Friars at Doncaster	12d.
The Carmelite Friars of York	12d.
Sisters Matilda and Eliste	6s. 8d.
Blessed Mary of Bradford	40s.

Dom William Scholes Chaplain – 6 of my best cups, a cloak of wool with fur and all my books.

Bradford Church gained independency from Dewsbury Minster and became a parish. The new Parish of Bradford included all the manors in Bradford Dale. Though these were independent manors they did not have a church so every Sunday their inhabitants were expected to travel to Bradford Parish Church for the services. This could be a long and arduous journey especially in bad weather. People were fined if they did not attend church. Outlying areas began to grumble about this inconvenience and a solution had to be reached. Churches were to be built in faraway areas of the dale so that parishioners would not have to undertake long journeys to worship. These were known as Chapels of Ease as they were easier to get to than the parish church. They were not parish churches. They were daughter churches of the Bradford Parish Church and the vicar of Bradford was vicar of these churches. As the vicar could not conduct services at all these chapels each Sunday a curate was put in charge. They were known as perpetual curates as they could not become vicars unless they moved to a parish church. These curates took the normal Sunday services, christened children and buried the dead but were not allowed to conduct marriages. Marriages were solemnised by the Vicar of Bradford either at the Bradford Parish Church or at the relevant Chapel of Ease.

Haworth Parish Church at the time of the Brontes from "A Spring-time Saunter" by Whiteley Turner.

The first recorded Chapel of Ease in the Bradford Parish was at Haworth in the 14th century when the state religion was still Roman Catholicism. In 1317, the Archbishop of York commanded the Vicar of Bradford to pay the Curate of Haworth his dues. A new chapel was constructed in 1488 and there have been at least two rebuilds since. Patrick Bronte was Perpetual Curate here from 1820 until he died in 1861.

Thornton Parish Church at the time of the Brontes from "The Brontes" by William Scruton

The second recorded Chapel of Ease was at Thornton. There was a chapel here in the 16th century after the Reformation and it was known as St Leonards. The church kept this name until 1612. In 1611, the new translation of the Bible known as the King James Bible was published. A new chapel was being **built** in Thornton due the generosity of ladies such as Precilla Bannister and it was decided to use a different name. In honour of the new bible translation it was named St James but was commonly known as the Bell Chapel. This again came under the rule of Bradford Parish Church and had a perpetual curate. Patrick Bronte officiated here from 1815 to 1820.

Holy Trinity Low Moor   *J C Senior*

The third recorded Chapel of Ease was at Low Moor. Holy Trinity Church, originally called Wibsey Chapel, was built in 1606 and consecrated in 1636. This was a Chapel of Ease for the people of the Royds and Bierley Estates in south Bradford. It was built on land donated by William Rookes of Royds Hall with extra money provided by Richard Richardson of Bierley Hall. Richardson also donated two oil paintings to be displayed in the chancel of the chapel.

The fourth recorded Chapel of Ease was at Bierley. After many years of harmony Richard Richardson (a descendent of the Richard Richardson involved in the establishment of Wibsey Chapel) and Edward Rookes (the last of the Rookes of Royds Hall) had a disagreement. Rookes withdrew permission for the people of the Bierley Estate to pass through the Royds Estate to worship at Wibsey Chapel. So, Richardson decided to construct his own Chapel of Ease. The Chapel of St John the Evangelist designed by John Carr of York was opened in 1766. It is the only Georgian Anglican Church in the Bradford Parish. Richardson decided his ancestor's paintings from Wibsey Chapel should be in his new chapel. Taking some of his men with him, Richardson broke into Wibsey Chapel, stole the paintings and took them to his new chapel where they hang, near the altar, to this day.

St John's Bierley   J C Senior

The income of the Bradford Parish Church was diverse and substantial. A great deal of the wealth came from the Glebe Lands. They were areas of land within an ecclesiastical parish which were used to support the parish priest. In the 17th century Bradford Glebe lands covered approximately 118 acres and included woodland, farms and farmland, mills and houses. The areas included were mainly in Undercliffe, Cliffe Woods and Goodman's End (the area at the bottom of the present Wakefield Road where the Exchange Station was built). The parsonage was in Goodman's End until the 19th century. Most of the Glebe Lands were sold in 1794 to such Bradford business families as the Hustlers and the Peckovers.

Another source of income was the Tithe where a percentage of produce or money was paid to the parish church each year. The estimated tithe income for 1638 from the Bradford Parish was £4012. Often the total collected fell below what was expected. It was difficult to administer, and many people objected to the arrangement especially with rise of non-conformity. People did not feel they should pay money to support a church they did not attend. The money was collected in the different manors scattered throughout the ecclesiastical parish. This is a list of what should have been collected in that year.

Bradford	£590	Parsonage (Lands)	£1332
Manningham	£450	Bolling	£404
Eccleshill	£120	Shipley	£79

Hortons	£603	Haworth	£200
Wibsey	£101	Allerton	£82
Thornton	£345		

Added to this were the Easter Tithes. 2d had to be paid for every person in a household over 16 years of age and ½d if a house had a chimney. The final insult was a 1d tithe on a family's garden.

Small tithes provided the vicar with food as well as money and must have been a further drain on many of the parishioners. A family keeping cattle were badly hit. For every seventh calf born 8 groats were to be paid. For every cow that had calved four times 3½d had to be paid. For every cow that had not calved 1d was due. It was no better if you kept pigs or fowls. One piglet out of a litter of six went to the vicar or 1d had to be paid if there were five or under in the litter. The vicar could take a goose or a turkey whenever he wished. The vicar was never without eggs as he could claim 1 egg for every hen and 2 for every cock. Horses were essential for transport and work, but the vicar still claimed 3 ½ d for every foal born. Keeping bees also brought a charge. If you had 7 hives one belonged to the vicar.

Then there were the Surplice Fees. Marriages, which could only be solemnised by the vicar and not a perpetual curate, were 5s for the license, 6d for the banns and 1s on the day. Burials, which could be carried out by the perpetual curate, were 5 groats for the service and 10d to dig the grave. A woman going to church for churching paid 6d. There were 14 corn mills in the Bradford Parish and 6 paid tithes to the church – Great Horton Mill, Sam's Mill in Horton, Leaventhorpe Mill, Dixon's Mill at Shipley, Thornton Mill and New Mill in Wilsden.

A great source of income to the vicar of Bradford was Pew Rentals. This was a system which began in the 14th century and by the 18th century was firmly established. Most pews within a church were rented by wealthier parishioners and just a few - 2were left for those who could not afford to pay. Some people believed they owned the pews they rented and tried to leave them to their heirs in their wills. Others acquired several pews and then sublet them at a tidy profit! These were the pew rents at the Bradford Parish Church in 1705. It is per seat not per pew.

Bradford	150 seats	3d to 8s
Horton	76 seats	3d to 9s 9d
Manningham	48 seats	3d to 4s
Heaton	20 seats	3d to 3s
Bowling	23 seats	3d to 5s
Wibsey & Bierley	18 seats	3d to 19s
Eccleshill	22 seats	2d to 6s
Shipley	16 seats	3d to 3s
Allerton	27 seats	3d to 2s 6d
Clayton	30 seats	3d to 3s 9d
Thornton	60 seats	3s to 4s
Wisden	23 seats	3d to 3s
Haworth	11 seats	9d to 5s
Oxenhope	30 seats	6d to 4s
Stanbury	11 seats	1s to 3s.

The closing years of Stuart Bradford saw the rise of non-conformity in the town bringing many changes in people's attitude to religion and caused a quickening of fear within the established church. Over the next two centuries the influence of the parish church was continually challenged, and Bradford became a northern stronghold for non-conformity.

GLOSSARY

Minster – Originally a form of monastic building by the eleventh century it was used for any church with an Anglo-Saxon foundation. In the twenty-first century, large parish churches have become minsters (e.g. Halifax and Leeds).

Churching - A blessing in church for a new mother after she had recovered from giving birth to a child.

Honor – The manors owned by a great lord which covered a wide area.

Patronage – The right to present or appoint a priest to a parish church.

Parish Clerk – An assistant to a parish priest who had not taken religious orders. Assisted at services and collected monies due to the church.

Tithe – A tenth of the profits of land and labour due to the parish church from every adult in the parish.

Surplice Fees – Fees paid to the parish priest when he performed baptisms, marriages or burials.

REFERENCES

All the books used for chapter one.

Bradford Directories in the BLSL

Alvin, Norman – Bradford Essays, BLSL B0012ALV

Documents relating to the Bradford Parish Church, BLSL 8283OUT

Faull & Stimson – Domesday Book Yorkshire, Parts 1&2 1986

CHAPTER THREE

JONATHAN GLYDE

Glyde House takes its name from this gentleman. The owners of the building asked me to research his life and work in Bradford. He is one of the many worthy citizens of this town, who contributed to its welfare and prosperity, that have no public memorial. I hope this article will go some way towards rectifying the omission.

Opposite the Ice Rink in Little Horton Lane is an imposing building named Glyde House.

Glyde House Bradford   *J C Senior*

This edifice is the only reminder left of what was once known as the "Non-Conformist Cathedral of Bradford". Until 1950 Glyde House accommodated the Sunday School of Horton Lane Congregational Church. Why Glyde House? It is named after the Reverend Jonathan Glyde who was, from 1835 to 1854, a much loved and respected minister of the first church which stood on this site.

Before looking at the life, work and influence of this charismatic man it is important to delve into the development of non-conformity in town. The burial records of the Society of Friends, commonly known as Quakers, record that they were in the town by 1656. The Quakers had several burial grounds one of which was at Goodman's End in 1672. They built meeting rooms there in 1710. Unitarians are known to have been in Bradford by 1688 as they built their first church at Chapel Green Little Horton then on land donated by the Puritan Thomas Sharp of Horton Hall in his will. The Moravians are recorded in Little Horton in 1742 and had a meeting room at Great Horton in 1745. The Moravian church at Lower Wyke was built in 1753. John Wesley preached in Little Horton in 1744 and an octagonal chapel was erected at Horton in 1776. Wesley preached at its opening and recorded the details in his journal. Baptists held their early meetings in a room at the Cockpit Inn in Westgate around 1753 after the private house they had been using from 1751 became too small. They built their first church in Westgate in 1755.

In the latter quarter of the 18th century under the leadership of a new minister, the Rev John Dean, the Unitarian Chapel in Little Horton became a Presbyterian Church. Several of the congregation were not happy at this move and left the church. They began to meet in one another's houses and looked around for suitable premises to start a new church. Mr James Garnett who lived in the Paper Hall allowed them to use a room for worship. Before long they had attracted so many to their services they needed new larger premises. The Old Brewery at the bottom of Horton Lane provided a suitable room that had housed malt. This sufficed until sufficient money had been raised to build a purpose-built chapel. By 1783 enough money had been raised to acquire land and build what became Horton Lane Independent (later Congregational) Chapel.

The Horton Lane Chapel from "Pen and Pencil Pictures of Old Bradford" by William Scruton

They built a chapel, a manse and a burial ground adjoining the dam of Rand's Mill. In 1824 Rand extended his mill by filling in the dam and putting the new building adjacent to, and overshadowing, the chapel.

This was the church that Jonathan Glyde was called to be minister at on 3rd December 1835. Jonathan was born into an old Dissenting family in Exeter in 1808. He was ordained an Independent minister in 1832 just one month before he married Miss Elizabeth Hull Terrell. Jonathan and Elizabeth were not blessed with children. Jonathan's mother died when he was 17 and father when he was 20. He became the guardian of his 2 surviving brothers. Jonathan's sisters were **looked after** by a maiden aunt. When he came to Bradford to "preach for a view" his wife and brothers stayed in Exeter.

Jonathan wrote to Elizabeth

Look which way, you will see huge tall chimneys poring forth volleys of smoke which, when you are near, is not pleasant but, when you see from a distance, is interesting enough. There cannot be fewer than a hundred of these chimneys in Bradford and its vicinity: a cloud therefore is continually hanging over it and this, together with the furnaces of the ironworks on the neighbouring hills the flames of which though not visible by day become bright by night, have led me to think that Bradford must be a very favoured spot having, like the children of Israel, its cloud by day and its fire by night.

Jonathan had two brothers, Lavington born in 1823 and William Evans born in 1814. Lavington lived with Jonathan and Elizabeth, working as a worsted spinner until he emigrated to Australia in 1850. There he became a Liberal MP and died in 1890. Lavington was responsible for introducing income tax to the country. William Evans also came to Bradford and began to work for the Salt family. He was at one time a director with Titus Salt and was greatly involved with the foundation of the Congregational Chapel in Saltaire. There is a plaque to him in the entrance foyer of the chapel.

The chapel that Jonathan came to as minister was attended by the "great and good" of the town. Titus Salt was a deacon and Sunday school teacher. The congregation included such local notables as William Byles, proprietor of the "Bradford Observer", James Garnett owner of Barkerend Mills, Samuel Smith owner of Horton Dyeworks and Robert Milligan Stuff Merchant Hall Ings. In 1850, of the 14 Bradford Aldermen 9 were members of the Horton Lane Chapel congregation. Jonathan was able by his character, example and rhetoric to influence the fate of his adopted town.

What was his influence on Bradford? Robert Blargarnie in his book on Sir Titus Salt wrote

The Reverend Jonathan Glyde by his mental culture and earnest piety exerted an influence over all with whom he ***came into contact. Mr Salt was one who felt this influence.***

Sir Titus Salt from "Pen and Pencil Portraits of Old Bradford" by William Scruton

Titus Salt is celebrated worldwide for his creation of the model industrial village of Saltaire. This massive venture began in 1851 sixteen years after he had met Jonathan and after sixteen years of sharing his friend's beliefs and dreams. Jonathan opinions were often aired in the local newspapers either in reports of his speeches at meetings or letters to the press. He once wrote

We must have schools of design and literary institutions, museums and music halls. We must have cottages better constructed and more capable of perfect ventilation, streets and courts cleaner and smelling a sweeter odour.

We must have baths and wash -houses and above all we must have a cemetery.

Is it a coincidence that the founders of Saltaire and Ripleyville were both worshippers at Horton Lane Chapel? Is not the above a description of Titus Salt's vision for his new village?

But Jonathan's influence extended beyond his congregation into the very life of the city. The middle of the 19th century showed a rise in the movement for public parks in the emerging industrial towns. Bradford had its own Parks Movement and Jonathan, along with Titus Salt, was an original member. Bradford Peel Park was opened in 1853.

Postcard of Peel Park from the author's private collection

In the same year, Jonathan had written

The town has risen from the smallest to one of the largest in the kingdom, but it has no large open market place, no broad greens no breathing places. If other towns have parks and pleasure grounds Bradford ought not to be without them. They are essential for health, cheerfulness and bodily and mental vigour. Exercise is essential to health of body and mind.

Mechanics' Institute from BLSL photographic collection

Bradford Mechanics' Institute opened in Leeds Road in 1840. Jonathan often lectured there, and his support was acknowledged after his death by the committee of the Institute. Throughout his ministry, Jonathan urged the adoption of education for all:

The battle of knowledge and virtue must be fought against ignorance, intemperance and vice.

The congregation at Horton Lane Chapel, under Jonathan's direction, worked tirelessly to erect and support the Borough West Schools in Horton. These schools opened in 1843, provided a non-denominational education for boys and girls from the age of 4 to 13 years. The schools continued even after the 1871 Education Act was passed, and Horton Lane Chapel held many events to raise the funds to make the schools successful.

Bradford West Schools from BLSL photographic collection

As Jonathan said

The welfare of the nation depends to a great extent on the education given to children and young persons. It is advisable that the religious instruction communicated in public schools should be free from sectarian peculiarities.

In 1849 Jonathan wrote

A fearful proportion of our fellow townsmen are living in neglect of all religious opportunities.... a deep and painful sense of immorality and irreligion pervades the masses of our fellow citizens.

Along with ministers from all religious sections of the town Jonathan created the Bradford Town Mission. People were employed to act as "missionaries" in the town arranging cottage meetings for prayer and bible classes and evening classes in reading and writing. The charity would provide food and clothing but never gave money to the poor for fear of misuse. After his death, the Committee wrote in their minutes that they

Acknowledge with devout thankfulness to Almighty God the services he (Rev Jonathan Glyde) was enabled to render the Mission as one of the most active in its organisation and much devoted to its support.

In 1853 Jonathan's health began to deteriorate. He resigned as minister in early 1854 and died in December of that year. His funeral service was conducted at Horton Lane Chapel before a large congregation made up of family, regular worshippers, town dignitaries and fellow ministers. The procession formed with hundreds of people on foot preceding the hearse whilst the congregation followed in carriages. A reporter in the "Bradford Observer" wrote

Many of the shops along the line of the route were closed.... the walk to the cemetery was exceedingly difficult. At the bottom of the grave were strewn some beautiful flowers.

Jonathan is buried in Undercliffe Cemetery. He was a modest man who by thoughtful Christian teaching and an exemplary life style enhanced the life of his adopted town. Whether his

Grave of Revd. Jonathan Glyde at Undercliffe Cemetery

J C Senior

influence on people such as Sir Titus Salt resulted in their later action it is impossible to say but he must have planted ideas that later grew to reality. It is a great sadness that there is no public recognition of this minister in the city today and that most of Bradford's citizens have no idea of his existence.

By his erudition, high culture, penetrating insight into human life and large grasp of affairs he was clothed with a strength and authority of character that he was universally acknowledged and deferred to. His purity of mind, his gentle spirit, his humanity, his sympathy with the young manhood, *his love of children gave him a rare place and hold on the affections of all who knew him.*

Horton Lane Chapel Centenary Memorial 1883.

Everything I have read about this man has praised his qualities of faith, his work ethic, his fine character and his total commitment to the spiritual, moral, educational and bodily welfare of the people of his adopted city.

William Cudworth 1889

GLOSSARY

Non-conformity – Any Protestant foundation not based on Anglican principles

Society of Friends or Quakers – Principal belief that it is possible to have a direct relationship with God without a priest.

Unitarianism – Principal belief that the Holy Trinity does not exist, and that God is one being. Jesus was a human being and not a deity.

Puritanism – Principal belief that the Anglican church needed to be purified from Catholic practices especially rich church ornamentation.

Moravians – This was the first Protestant church to be founded. Principal beliefs were that services should not be in Latin, priests should be able to marry and the selling of indulgencies to cease.

Baptists – Principal belief that infant baptism is wrong. Baptism should be total immersion for adult believers.

Presbyterianism – Originated in Scotland. Principal belief that the individual churches should be governed by a group of elders.

Congregationalism – Principal belief that it is the right and responsibility of each properly organised congregation to determine its own affairs.

REFERENCES

Horton Lane Independent Chapel Records, WYAS Bradford, 5D74

Memoirs and remains of the late Rev Jonathan Glyde, Pastor of Horton Lane Chapel   1858

Balgarnie, Robert - Sir Titus Salt, Baronet: His life and its lessons
                                                                                    1877

Scruton, William -   Pen and Pencil Sketches of Old Bradford
                                                                                    1889

English Census details   1841-1851 from ancestry.com

CHAPTER FOUR

BRADFORD AND THE PARKS MOVEMENT

As the previous chapter pointed out we have many things good about our city that we owe to people such as Jonathan Glyde. Our parks are jewels in the towns' possession and hopefully will long remain so.

In the middle of the 19th century, when the Rev. Jonathan Glyde was the minister at Horton Lane Chapel, Bradford was not a picturesque, healthy or well-planned town. Visitors to the town were unimpressed and reported to the world the town's shortcomings.

Drawing of Frederick Engels by Mary Tetlow

Frederick Engels wrote after visiting the town

Bradford lies upon the banks of a small coal-black foul-smelling stream. On week-days the town is enveloped in

a grey cloud of coal smoke. In the valley reigns filth and discomfort. In the lanes, alleys and courts lie filth and debris.

(Conditions of the Working Class in England 1844)

Drawing of Georg Weerth by Mary Tetlow

Georg Weerth wrote after visiting the town

Bradford is the most disgusting manufacturing town in England. It is dirty, foggy, smelly and cold. Every other English industrial centre is a paradise compared with this filthy hole. There can be no doubt whatever that here in Bradford one is living in the very home of Lucifer himself.
(Letters home 1843-1846)

Prominent people within the town, such as the Revd. Jonathan Glyde and Titus Salt, were anxious to improve the living and working conditions of the town's inhabitants. For Titus Salt this concern resulted in the creation of Saltaire. But Jonathan Glyde wanted the improvements to be within the town itself.

In 1853, this plea from Jonathan Glyde was printed in the Bradford Observer

Bradford has come from one of the smallest to one of the largest in the kingdom, but it has no open market place, no broad greens and no breathing places. Parks are essential for health, cheerfulness and bodily and mental vigour. Exercise is essential to the health of body and mind. The working class needs space for running, leaping, tumbling, dancing, games and sports of all kinds.

At the start of the 19th century there were no free public parks in England. The aristocracy had their large estates surrounded by parkland, but the general public could be prosecuted if they dared to visit without, rarely given, permission. There were recreation parks, such as the Vauxhall Gardens in London, where entertainments were provided, but the admission charge precluded most of the population visiting them.

A Government Select Committee was organised in 1840 to investigate the Health of Towns. This Committee found that Bradford was not alone in suffering worrying conditions. Among the Select Committee's proposals, for the improvement of health in towns, was the provision of free open spaces. The Government set up a framework for the provision of public parks and £10,000 towards this was allocated in 1841. The first free accessible public park was opened in Birkenhead in 1844.

Titus Salt first suggested a public park for Bradford when he was mayor in 1849. It took until 1850 before the decision was taken to have a privately funded public park. This was to be a public memorial to Sir Robert Pee,l a great supporter of the Free Trade Movement, and considered a hero by many Bradfordians.

Titus Salt and Robert Milligan from "Historical Notes on the Bradford Corporation" by William Cudworth

Titus Salt and Robert Milligan, another former mayor, started the fund and it was expected that there would soon be sufficient money to begin construction. Bradford was divided into districts and people employed to collect the money. By 1853 there was sufficient money available to purchase land in Undercliffe and work began. For the first few years the park was supported by public funds, but the flow of money slowed, and the Committee decided to hand the park over to the Bradford Corporation in 1863.

Titus Salt had allowed some of his wool combers to work as navvies on the site for which he had to pay a surety of £100.

By 1854 there were reports of thefts and vandalism of building materials so two watchmen were appointed. When the lake was constructed James Hill, another mayor of Bradford, presented two swans. Every year at Whitsuntide a fund-raising event was held at the park when the citizens of Bradford had to pay an entrance fee. Bradford applied to the Government for a grant to help with the building costs. The town was granted £1,500 on the proviso that

The park is secured legally and permanently as a place of recreation for the inhabitants of Bradford.

There were strict rules and regulations, drawn up in 1859, which had to be followed.

1. The gates are to be opened at 6 am in summer and sunrise in winter.

2. The gates are to be closed at sunset in both summer and winter.

3. The closing time will be signalled by the ringing of a bell and visitors must leave immediately.

4. Visitors will be fined 40/- if found picking flowers, damaging plants shrubs or trees, or in any way defacing or injuring the grounds.

5. No intoxicating liquors are to be taken into the park.

6. No dogs are allowed.

7. No standing on the seats in the Swiss Cottage

8. Anyone cutting names into the fabric or furniture of the Swiss Cottage will be fined.

9. Please keep off the grass or you will spoil the beauty and freshness.

10. The Committee hope that the public will respect that which is provided for the public accommodation.

11. The Committee hope that the public will protect that which is intended for the public enjoyment.

Peel Park postcard from author's private collection

After the success of the creation of Peel Park the Bradford Corporation began to construct public parks through-out the town. The parks were deliberately planned to circle the town so that each area's population had access to a free open space. They were not placed in the valley bottom but on the slopes overlooking the town centre and hopefully above the worst smoke pollution. All the parks had a park keeper, a gardener and under-gardeners to look after them. They all also had same ten elements:

1. A promenade

2. Flower gardens, shrubs and trees

3. Seating areas

4. Greenhouses

5. A refreshment area

6. Drinking fountains

7. A band stand

8. A park keeper's lodge

9. Gates and walls

10. A lake

Though greatly altered over the following years the five Victorian parks constructed by the Bradford Council are all still available to the population for recreational activities. Four of these parks are Grade II listed and are on the list of English Heritage's Historic Parks.

The first listed park was the afore mentioned Peel Park which opened in 1853. The park gates and lodges also have listed building status. Peel Park's lake is a distorted figure-of-eight shape. There is a fountain dedicated to the Band of Hope which was situated on Manningham Lane until 1861. At the side of the lake are the only remains of the Old Bradford Manor House which stood in Kirkgate. The manor house was built by the Rawson family in 1705 but was demolished in 1870 when Kirkgate Market was built. The doorway and the inscription describing when the manor house was built and by whom was included into the attractions of the new park.

Statue of Sir Robert Peel in Peel Park   J C Senior

On the promenade is a statue of Robert Peel moved there from Peel Square in 1926. There are sweeping lawns, flower beds, trees and bushes. One area is a designated play area. Peel Park has retained its greenhouses and supplies plants for the city's flower beds and official functions at the City Hall.

The second listed park to be built was in Manningham. It was on the site of the Manningham Hall estate of Samuel Cunliffe Lister. When Lister moved to Masham he put the estate up for sale and Bradford bought it at a reduced price. The park was opened in 1870 and named Lister Park after the former owner. Manningham Hall was demolished and some of the stone used to construct the Norman Arch. Lister Park is also on the English Heritage register of Historic Parks. There are seven grade two listings for this park (the park, the statue of Lister erected 1875, the statue of Salt moved here in 1896, the gates, the lodges, Cartwright Hall 1904 and Norman Arch 1903)

Postcard of Lister Park gates from the author's private collection.

The lake was the first feature to be constructed. It is serpentine in shape, with four islands, and was originally a boating lake with a boating shed. The meteorological station, which is still in operation, was opened in 1908 and sends information daily to the Met Office and the local papers. Lister Park has many interesting features which make it the most visited Park in Bradford. The Art Gallery based at Cartwright **Hall continually** displays world renowned exhibitions. The Botanical Gardens, which were designed in 1903, was replanted in 1953 on a "Themed Basis" to show the plants used in the textile industry.

There is a Sensory Garden where visitors can smell the scents of different flowers and feel the textures of different plants.

When it came to providing the third park, which was for Little and Great Horton, there was a shortage of money and land. This park had to be long and thin to fit the space. Horton Park is the third of Bradford Parks to be listed and placed on the English Heritage's Register of Historic Parks and Gardens. The main feature of this park is its two lakes with a bridge walk between them. Part of the old Bradford Dungeon is set into the side of the lower lake. The dungeon was situated at the top of Ivegate and stretched under the road. Originally the park had a circular pond with a fountain. The pond has been filled in and the fountain no longer functions. There are no statues in this park.

Postcard of Horton Park Lake from the author's private collection

The fourth listed park, opened in 1880, was in Bowling and caused problems due to the steepness of the land and the prevailing winds. The land, purchased from the Bolling Hall Estate, was terraced in places to provide different areas of interest. The original plans by Kershaw and Hepworth of Brighouse included a croquet lawn and a reservoir. However, these plans were not used. A small stream flowed down the western side of the park interspersed with small ponds. This area also included the Hot House greenhouses providing the locals with the experience of exotic plants not available to many. Later, at the side of the children's play area, a paddling pool was constructed. The northern area of the park became a miniature golf course where many young Bradfordians were introduced to the sport. At the northern edge of the park is Bowling Cemetery on land purchased at the same time as the park.

Postcard of Bowling Park from the author's private collection

This park is also Grade ii listed and is on the English Heritage Register of Parks and Gardens of Historic Interest. There is a drinking fountain dedicated to Councillor John Johnson who represented the East Bowling Ward. On the 2[nd]October 1893 he contracted smallpox whilst helping to rescue patients from the temporary Isolation Hospital at Scholemoor. Johnson helped carry 55 patients to safety before the wooden building was destroyed. He later died. Bowling Park, Horton Park and Lister Park all have a fossilised tree trunk in their grounds. These fossils were discovered in a quarry at Clayton and were donated by the quarry owners to the Bradford Council to place in public places.

Postcard of Bradford Moor Park from the author's private collection.

The last of Bradford's Victorian parks was at Bradford Moor and is one of the smallest to be constructed. It opened in 1884 and is not listed. It had a large lake which was used for sailing model boats, a bowling green and a bandstand. Soldiers were based at the Bradford Moor Barracks adjoining the park. This area became their main recreation place. Their military band often played in the bandstand.

At the same time as providing the city with Public Parks the Council realised areas were also needed for organised physical games. Many of the recreational grounds used today by local football, rugby, hockey and cricket teams owe their existence to the forward thinking of Victorian forefathers.

REFERENCES

Bills, receipts etc. concerning Peel Park, 1842-1886,   WYAS Bradford 11D74/3/88

Alvin, Norman - Open Spaces for the Humbler Classes BHAS Antiquary Series 3 volume 17   2013

Bentley, Joseph - Illustrated Handbook of the Bradford City Parks, Recreational Grounds and Open Spaces   1926

City of Bradford MDC   Parks on www.bradford.gov.uk

CHAPTER FIVE

THE 1851 RELIGIOUS CENSUS

This talk was composed for the first Bradford Historical and Antiquarian Society Day School held at the Bradford Club in 2015. It has never been used at Glyde House, but I often refer to this census when looking at religious institutions in Victorian England.

In the middle of the nineteenth century, the Registrar General, Major George Gordon, decided the country needed a more extensive statistical investigation than the ten-yearly population census provided. He decided on three different census forms; the general population census, an education census and a religious census. Due to the extra work and expense involved the education and religious census were not repeated.

Why was a religious census considered necessary? The British Government was concerned at the state of religion in the country. The established state church was the Church of England. Ministers were concerned that it was losing its influence with the working population of the country. There was much civil unrest and a large growth in non-conformity. These were all worrying signs for a government concerned about the revolutionary events happening on the continent and in the New World. Many questioned whether or not it was an invasion of privacy, especially for the middle and upper classes.

So how was the Religious Census to be carried out? The Census Enumerators for each district of Bradford supplied the names and addresses of the minister or person responsible for each religious congregation in the city. Each person on that list was sent a form with instructions to complete it on Sunday the 30th March 1851. The forms had to be returned to the Enumerator by the end of Monday 31st March 1851.

What did the form look like?

1. The name and address of the religious establishment.

2. The date of the construction of the building.

3. The cost of its erection and where the money for its construction came from.

4. The attendance on 30th March 1851 at morning, afternoon and evening services for both the General Congregation and the Sunday School.

5. The average attendance over the last year.

6. Any endowments that were due to the church. Number of Trustees.

7. Minister and any others responsible for the running of the church.

8. Remarks by the person completing the form.

The 1851 Census forms were completed by eleven different religious sects within the city of Bradford showing the diversity that is still reflected today.

Christian Brethren	1 meeting place
Society of Friends	1 meeting place
Roman Catholic	1 meeting place
Temperance Movement	1 meeting place
Latter Day Saints	2 meeting places
Moravians	2 meeting places
Presbyterian	3 meeting places
Baptist	10 meeting places
Independent	12 meeting places
Church of England	21 meeting places
Methodist (all types!)	53 meeting places

Most ministers tried to complete the forms conscientiously, but many failed to understand the instructions given. There are a suspicious number of rounded up figures. As there was no legal requirement to complete the form a substantial number of Anglican clergy did not return the forms, among these was the vicar of Bradford Parish Church the Rev John Burnet.

The remarks section was usually completed by people showing their dissatisfaction with the whole process. Few leaders of the congregations show any support for the investigation. Many took the opportunity to air grievances that had no bearing on the questions asked. On reading the remarks it is obvious the weather on the 30th March 1851 was stormy and affected the attendance numbers at several the more isolated meeting places

First Westgate Baptist Chapel from "Jubilee Album of Old Bradford Views" *William Cudworth*

At Westgate Baptist Chapel 1,883 worshippers attended the three general services and 511 attended the Sunday School meetings. Rev Henry Dowson obviously thought little of the contents of the form or the task to be undertaken. He wrote

These numbers have been accurately counted. In all cases where the congregation is taken by estimate the number is sure to be overestimated. There is nothing so deceptive as it regards numbers as the appearance of public assemblies. In connection with this congregation, there are four Sabbath Schools supported by voluntary contributions and one day School. The whole sustained without any aid from government

Independent Chapel Denholme   *J C Senior*

At the Independent Chapel Denholme 355 worshippers attended the services and 137 the Sunday School meeting. Ebenezer Heron the minister was concerned his low congregation numbers would reflect on him, so he wrote

Both congregation and School are at present beneath the average on account of fever being prevalent in the Hamlet.

Wesleyan Reformers met at the Hall of Refuge. One thousand worshippers attended two general services and two hundred attended the Sunday School meetings. William Savage one of the Local Ministers & Leaders decided to air his dissatisfaction with the conduct of the Wesleyan movement in Bradford. He wrote

The service conducted in this place is on account of the tyrannical proceedings of the Wesleyan preachers in the Bradford West Circuit in expelling members, leaders and preachers simply because they are anxious to have certain popish innovations expunged from our Wesleyan church policy. Services are conducted by a number of expelled Local Ministers or Preachers.

Christ Church, Church of England, located at the top of Darley Street (since demolished), was a popular church and served a large area. On the 30th March 2,100 attended the three general services and 1,800 the Sunday School meetings. The minister, at that time, was the Revd. William Morgan, a friend of Rev Patrick Bronte.

Christ Church from "Jubilee Album of Old Bradford Views"

The Revd. Morgan wrote

Railway travelling lessens the attendance in the afternoon as do pleasure gardens. The weather, too, affects Yorkshire Congregations. We know friends lost by the letting of pews. Many other things might be said. I have filled up the form as well as I could, considering the shortness of time and smallness of space. I wish these queries had been drawn up by some more practical man than the Registrar and Secretary of State. The clergy too should have had a month at least to give full details and explanations and some account should have been desired and furnished of those who frequent no place of worship.

When the results of the census were published, they fuelled the rivalry between the Church of England and Non-Conformity. It is considered an important source of early Victorian life. The Yorkshire returns show the continuing influence of the Church of England in the countryside but a significant rise in Non-Conformity and religious indifference in the industrial towns.

What else did the results show? The population of England and Wales was more than the number of sittings available in Church of England buildings. Worshippers in Non-Conformist buildings outnumbered those attending Church of England services. The Church of England could no longer call itself the "national church". Church of England worship was strongest in London, the eastern counties and rural areas. Non-Conformity worship was strongest in the northern counties, the western counties and Wales.

What was Bradford's response the results? The religious leaders in Bradford were concerned at the large number of people who attended no form of worship at all. So, if people were not attending a service, then religion must be taken to the people. The Bradford Town Mission was quickly formed. It was not a building. The churches of all denominations joined together to employ missionaries to work amongst the most deserving. The missionaries offered support, education, clothing and food. Non-sectarian services were held in peoples' homes or in the open air. Rooms were hired so classes in reading, writing and numeracy could be held. Parents were encouraged to send their children to school. Clothing and food banks were organised in the neediest areas.

How did the Anglican Church in Bradford react? The results horrified the Anglican clergy. Though they must have been aware of the rising number of Non-Conformists in the town these results made worrying reading for them. Applications were made to London for new Church of England churches to be established. In the next ten years

What do the results tell us about religion in Bradford in the middle of the 19th century? Most of the population of Bradford did not attend any form of organised religious worship and that this was across all social classes. People on low incomes stayed at home or enjoyed local facilities. People on higher incomes took advantage of the improved forms of public transport to journey outside the town. If people did attend some form of religious worship, it was more likely to be a Non-Conformist rather than an Anglican service. Religion was not important to most of the town's population. For many people, Sunday was becoming a day of rest, relaxation and catching up with household chores.

REFERENCES

Wolffe, John editor - Yorkshire Returns of the 1851 Census of Religious Worship Volume 1: Introduction, City of York and East Riding   2000

Wolffe, John editor - Yorkshire Returns of the 1851 Census of Religious Worship Volume 2: West Riding

CHAPTER SIX

CHARLES SAMUEL JOSEPH SEMON

This gentleman has long been of interest to me as my grandmother, my mother and myself have reasons to be thankful for his generosity to the people of Bradford.

For many years, people from all parts of the world have arrived in Bradford which they soon began to look upon as home. Today, many Bradfordians can trace their ancestry back to such countries as Italy, Germany, Poland, the Ukraine, Russia, Latvia, Estonia, Ireland, Pakistan, India, and the West Indies. The nineteenth century population growth of Bradford was partly due to the influx of displaced agricultural workers and people arriving from abroad.

German Jews came to Bradford from around 1820 onwards. Unlike later immigrants from Europe, they were not seeking freedom from persecution but rather to take advantage of expanding business opportunities and so make their fortunes. These men were not itinerant pedlars nor were they particularly religious. Many were already successful business men in their own country but looked upon Bradford as a place to excel. They were to have a great influence on the city and helped turn it into a major commercial centre. Once settled in the city these entrepreneurs made sure they contributed in all areas of their adopted city's development. One of the first to settle in Bradford was Jacob Behrens. In 1836 he founded a factory on Thornton Road and used his resultant wealth to benefit the city. Behrens was one of the founder members of the Bradford Chamber of Commerce, a Trustee of the Bradford Boys Grammar School, a supporter of the Bradford Technical College and a Trustee of the Eye and Ear Hospital.

Postcard of the Bradford Technical College from author's private collection.

These German merchants were responsible for the wonderful warehouse buildings in Little Germany. They had their own club, Schiller Veriin, where they would meet for a liquid lunch before returning to their offices to sleep off the after effects!

By 1873 the numbers of German Jews in the city had greatly increased and a Jewish Association was formed.

To uphold and advance the cause of Judaism and provide for the religious teaching of Jewish children.

It was not until the 1870s that a permanent synagogue was opened in Boland Street. Before then, their services were first held in the Masonic Lodge in Salem Street and then the Unitarian Chapel in Town Hall Square. In 1877, a section of

Scholemoor cemetery was purchased to create a Jewish burial ground.

Warehouse in Little Germany   *J C Senior*

Charles Semon was amongst those responsible for the foundation of the Jewish Association and a leading figure in the Jewish community.

Charles Simon Joseph Semon was born in Danzig in 1814. At that time, Danzig was part of the kingdom of Prussia. His parents were middle class Jews and he enjoyed a safe and settled upbringing. Semon senior was a merchant and Charles was well educated. In his 20s he married Agnes Pick in Hamburg. The couple did not have any children. Charles was aware of England's industrial expansion and the opportunities for trade attracted him. In 1839, he sailed from Boulogne to

London with letters of introduction to Germans already settled in this country. One of these recommended connections was the firm of Schaub and Gobert in Bradford where Charles came to work. The firm had branches in Bradford and Manchester. After greatly impressing his new employers Charles was offered a managerial post in Manchester. However, he was determined to make his mark in this country and resigned from this role. He returned to Bradford and went into partnership with John Siltzer. They were stuff merchants based in Charles Street off Market Street. This partnership lasted for 15 years before it was dissolved in 1856. Charles spent a short time in London but found that it was really Bradford that could offer the opportunities he was looking for. He returned to the city and in 1847 began a new business in the Exchange Passage and then at 22 Church Bank where it remained for over 100 years.

Charles' firm prospered, and he traded with Australia, America, Europe and the Baltic States. His firm was at the forefront of the city's emerging international trade that contributed greatly to its importance in the 19th century. Charles' contribution to the health and welfare of the city was immeasurable. He diversified by buying property in Manningham and proved to be an excellent landlord. He also paid for road improvements in that area. Charles was a trustee of the Third Bradford Equitable Building Society; a governor of the Bradford Infirmary for 20 years; helped finance the introduction of the Eye and Ear hospital; a founder member of the Bradford Chamber of Commerce and Director of the Bradford Mechanics' Institute.

Charles Semon from Historical Notes on the Bradford Corporation William Cudworth

Charles' contribution to the prosperity of his adopted city was recognised in 1864 when he was elected, unopposed, as mayor. The outgoing mayor Alderman Godwin said

The wool trade has been represented by the spinning and manufacturing and home merchants have also been represented. Our great staple trade, the largest branch being that of the export trade has never been represented.

We can lay our hands on the right man for the right place.

In supporting the motion Alderman Thompson said

In electing him the council not only wished to honour him for his own deservings but to pay a compliment to the foreign merchants who contributed much to the prosperity of the borough.

Charles Semon holds the honour of being the Third elected Jewish Mayor in this country after London and Nottingham.

Drawing of Manningham Old Hall by Mary Tetlow

Charles and Agnes lived at the Lodge of Manningham Old Hall. After Agnes death, he married for a second time, in Leipzig, to Louise Johannes Angela Bressel von Bressendorf. The couple moved to Broughton Hall near Skipton in 1873. When his health deteriorated in 1876 Charles went to Switzerland where

he died in 1877. His body was returned to Bradford where he had a civic funeral.

A postcard of Bradford Town Hall from the author's private collection

The night before the funeral Charles' body lay in state in the Town Hall. The coffin was carried in procession along Market Street to Great Horton Road then to Shearbridge, Legrams Lane, Cemetery Road and finally the new Jewish area in the Scholemoor cemetery. Police lined the route and crowds stood in silence to watch the cortege pass by. Shops along the route were closed. The Town Hall bell tolled, and the chimes played Mendelssohn's "O Rest in the Lord". The hearse was followed by his work force, members of the town council, representatives of all organisations he was involved with, members of the Jewish Association, family and friends. At the cemetery was a table covered in a white cloth. On it was a box with the label "Remember the Poor". It was the second Jewish burial at the cemetery.

An honourable tribute to the genuine work of the deceased. A testimony to the esteem the deceased had won for himself from all classes of the community by his ostentatious generous support of all our benevolent institutions.

His readiness to respond to all appeals for help from whatever quarter once they proved themselves as deserving. His upright and consistent conduct as a man of business. His assiduous endeavours in a whole variety of ways to discharge to the utmost of his ability the duties falling on him as one of the foremost citizens of Bradford.

Before he died Charles had provided a Nursing Home in Ilkley which he gave to the Bradford Council in 1874.

The rules for acceptance were strictly adhered to.

The Nursing Home was for

Persons of slender means

Those in a weak state of health

Persons who had been ill and tardy in recovering.

The long list of those precluded from admittance show that many citizens of Bradford would not qualify for help.

It was not for

Persons who were blind, helpless or under 10 years of age

Persons recovering from smallpox, typhus and scarlet fever

Persons having open sores or a skin disease

Epileptics

Persons unsound of mind

Persons having cancer, tuberculosis or any incurable disease

Pregnant women

Persons on parochial relief.

Use of the facilities offered was not free of charge. It cost 12s 6d to stay for one week and the maximum stay was to be no more than 3 weeks. Patients were expected to take a change of underwear, a pair of boots and a pair of slippers. Any dirty clothes had to be taken away by relations who were expected to launder them.

Postcard of Semon Nursing Home from the author's private collection

The Nursing Home was known as Semon's Home and existed into the second half of the 20th century. During the 2nd World War it was used as a maternity Home for St Luke's Hospital patients. I was born there in 1945 and, during the 1960s, when it had become a convalescent home again, my grandmother spent two weeks there recovering from an operation.

Charles had also started an educational foundation. The Charles Semon Educational Foundation for the Free Grammar School of King Charles II at Bradford was established to

Provide education of persons under the age of 25, who are resident in the area of benefit ,by the provision of

1. Exhibitions and scholarships to Bradford Grammar School for pupils from any elementary school within the area.

2. Exhibitions and scholarships to higher education institutions for pupils from Bradford Grammar School.

The foundation is still in existence and pupils benefit from Charles' forethought each year.

This unassuming gentleman was welcomed to the city and he gladly made it his home, becoming a naturalised British citizen in his middle age. Charles used his business acumen not just for his own advancement but for the growth and welfare of his adopted town. So, how does the city of Bradford commemorate this former merchant and mayor who played such an important role in the growth of its prosperity?

Street name of Semon Avenue at Swaine House   *J C Senior*

REFERENCES

Cudworth, William - Historical notes on the Bradford Corporation   1881

Mr Smith, Bursar, Bradford Grammar School

English Census details 1861 to 1871, Ancestry.com

Bradford directories 1860 to 1870, BLSL

Burgess Rolls 1860 to 1876, BLSL

West Riding directories 1870-1876, BSLS

Semon Convalescents Home Ilkley, BLSL

Memorial in Scholemoor Cemetery for Charles Semon

J C Senior

CHAPTER SEVEN

FOREIGN CONSULS IN BRADFORD

Whilst working as a volunteer at the Local Studies Library, Bradford I came across some interesting newspaper cuttings. After some further research and with help from a librarian at the US Historic Records Department, this talk was prepared.

By the 1860s Bradford was entering a period of extreme prosperity, growth and influence. The easy access to coal, iron and soft water facilitated the expansion of Bradford as a manufacturing base. Improved roads and access to the national rail network eased the export of Bradford's products as the canal was falling into disuse.

An abundance of local sandstone helped with easing the cost of new buildings. The Wool Exchange, opened in 1867, provided a weekly market and meeting place for the numerous wool merchants based in the city and surrounding areas. The wonderful Italianate Town Hall was to open in 1873. Model villages had been constructed at Ripleyville, in 1866, and Saltaire, between 1853 and 1871, with advanced ideas on housing and amenities for workers in the textile industry. The cultural life of the city was catered for by the opening of St George's Hall in 1853, for musical performances, and the Prince's Theatre in 1876, for dramatic productions. A choral society was formed in 1853 which eventually became the Bradford Festival Choral Society. To cater for the less sophisticated interests, Henry Pullan opened a Music Hall in

Brunswick Place in 1869. By the end of the 1860s, local news was being provided by three Bradford newspapers, the *Bradford Daily Telegraph*, the *Bradford (Illustrated) Weekly Telegraph* and *the Bradford Observer*.

Building regulations in the town resulted in better working-class housing beginning to appear. However, it was to take many years before slum areas began to disappear. The Bradford Council began to discuss the necessity for a network of sewers and drains to alleviate the stench from unpaved streets and the stinking Beck which still ran openly through the middle of the city. Water was already being piped into the city from at least eleven reservoirs, but most people had no access to fresh water in their homes. It is not surprising that the two new parks, Peel Park 1853 and Manningham Park 1870, were extremely popular with Bradfordians anxious to escape the smells and smoke which surrounded their houses. For those who could afford to hire transport, or were energetic walkers, trips to Shipley Glen became a popular Sunday outing.

The influence of the German immigrants on the prosperity of Bradford at this period was of great significance. Due to their enterprise Bradford became an international city exporting and trading with all corners of the world. This importance was recognised by the countries Bradford traded with. During this expansion, Foreign Consular representation to the city began. One of the earliest consuls to open was that of the United States of America.

Between 1861 and 1865 the USA was torn apart by a brutal civil war. On one side were the eleven southern states who were called the Confederates. They wanted to keep the practice of slavery and lessen the control of the central government. On the other side were thirty-four states known as the Unionists. They wished to abolish slavery and keep the control of a central government.

Both sides wished to have British support. Cotton from the USA was an essential imported commodity, especially for the cotton mills of Lancashire. The Confederate States were the areas that produced the cotton for export. They stopped the export of cotton to England believing this country would support them to have the trade restarted. However, after a period of suffering by the cotton mills in Lancashire, England found other supplies from Egypt and India. Also, there was a very large and influential Anti-Slavery Movement in England and support for trade with a place where slavery continued was not forthcoming. The grain crops in England failed between 1860 to 1862. The Unionist states of the USA were the grain growing areas of that country and it was to them that England turned for help. To show their appreciation of this support, trade between the Unionist states expanded and the USA began to place consulates in what they considered were this country's major cities.

An American Consulate was opened in Bradford on December 6th, 1863 in a building on Cheapside.

Drawing of the USA Consulate

BLSL newspaper cuttings collection

It remained there until 1871 when it moved to the Exchange Buildings on Market Street. After Swan Arcade was constructed the consulate moved here in 1875 and remained there well into the twentieth century. The USA moved their consulate into Britannia House after the second world war where it remained until its closure in 1953. The first consular agent was John Emory McClintock, the son of a college tutor. Due to illness McClintock could not fight in the civil war so Lincoln appointed him to a consular post in Bradford where he remained until 1866. Consuls in the nineteenth century were involved in the issuing of licences for Bradford merchants to export goods to the USA. Most of Bradford's exports were woollen goods but the consular also issued licences for the export to the USA of grindstones, fireworks, hog bristle brushes, boot protectors and novelties for bird cages!

McClintock returned to Bradford from the USA in 1868 to marry Zoe Darlington the daughter of John Darlington.

It is not clear which was the first country to open a consulate in Bradford but is was most likely Belgium. Foreign countries often appointed Bradfordians to act as consular agents for them. John Darlington, Bradford's Superintendent Registrar, was approved as Belgian consular agent to Bradford by Queen Victoria on the 5th December 1862. By 1864 he was consular agent for Belgium, France, Italy and Serbia. In 1879 his son Latimer, a solicitor, was appointed consular agent for Spain. For his long service to Belgium, King Leopold made John Darlington a Knight of Leopold in 1881.

The extensive scope of Bradford's international trading partners was reflected in the visitors to the town.

Victoria Hotel Bradford   *J C Senior*

On the 1871 census there were thirteen foreign merchants staying at the Victoria Hotel. They came from France, Germany, USA, Turkey and Italy.

By 1879 eleven countries had some form of consular representation in Bradford and by 1901 this total had risen to fourteen:

A W Lassen	The Austro-Hungarian Empire
F Darlington	Belgium
C W Dunlop	Chile
A H Blankley	France
V Edelstein	The German Empire
F Darlington	Italy
S Vos	The Netherlands

D & R Delius	Norway
W Hertz	Portugal
F Darlington	Serbia
F Darlington	Spain
D & R Delius	Sweden
E S Day	United States of America
S Simon	Uruguay

Albert William Lassen lived at 2 Clifton Villas and was a wool tops and stuff merchant. Lassen was born in Bradford but his father was from Bavaria, Germany. Frank Darlington was another member of the Darlington family. Charles W Dunlop the agent for Chile was born in Scotland and was a woollen and stuff goods merchant living in Embsay near Skipton. Arthur H Blankley, agent for France, was a solicitor born in London and living in Ilkley. Victor Edelstein agent for the German Empire lived at 1 Oak Lane and he was a wool and yarn merchant. Edelstein was born in Germany. Simeon Vos, agent for the Netherlands, was a wool merchant living in St Paul's Road. Vos was born in Holland. The brothers Daniel and Rudolf Delius were both born in the kingdom of Prussia. They were wool merchants trading with the Baltic nations. Daniel lived in Selbourne Villas and Rudolf on St Paul's Road. Their nephew was Frederick Delius, the composer. William Hertz, agent for Portugal, was a stuff woollen merchant and lived in Oak Lane. Hertz's father was born in Hamburg Germany. The Manningham district of Bradford had quickly become the place where the middle classes wanted to live. It was also becoming the multi-cultural area of the city. On the 1901 census people from Sweden, Germany, France, Switzerland and Ireland were living on St Paul's Road.

St Paul's Road Manningham Bradford   J C Senior

The first world war changed the face of Europe and the international make-up of Bradford. By the end of 1916, the consuls of the Austro-Hungarian Empire, the German Empire, Chile and Uruguay had disappeared. The French consul, Claude Lievre had been in Bradford for nineteen years and was 43 years of age when war broke out. He was the proprietor of a language school and married to a local girl, Clare Varley. Lievre was still a French citizen although he was well established in the city even becoming a freemason in 1906. When war was declared, he was responsible for French subjects living in the area who wished to return to fight for their country. After two years of war he decided to enlist himself and left for France in 1916.

The situation of those people of German descent living in Bradford was now daunting. Many were naturalized British citizens but for many inhabitants they were still Germans and therefore the enemy. After the disbanding of the German consul the USA consular agent, Mr Ingram, assumed the protection of German subjects who wished to remain in Bradford. This situation continued until the USA entered the conflict in 1916. Ingram also kept records of all American subjects in the area as a preparation for what was seen by many as the inevitable involvement in the fighting of the USA. He was in Bradford for the duration of the war and remained as consular agent until 1920.

After 1918, some consuls reopened and by the start of the second world war in 1939 the number had risen to nineteen;

America	Argentina	Austria	Belgium
Denmark	Czechoslovakia	Finland	France

Germany	Greece	Italy	Latvia
Netherlands	Norway	Romania	Serbia
Spain	Sweden	Uruguay.	

Every year the consuls were invited to attend a civic reception at Bradford Town Hall. Each consulate flew its country's flag outside their consulate building. But Bradford's influence on the world stage was greatly diminished. The fate of consulate representation in Bradford reflects its economic and manufacturing decline. In 1953, there were only nine consulates and by 1960 this had been reduced further to six.

The huge growth in Bradford's population of people from the Asian subcontinent caused the Pakistan government to appoint a representative to the city in 1971. By 1975 a Pakistan consulate had opened in Cheapside. More consulates closed over the following years so that by the end of the twentieth century only four remained; Denmark, Italy, Norway and Pakistan. Of these the only one remaining in 2017 was the Pakistan consulate

Pakistan Consulate Bradford   J C Senior

The early foreign consuls in Bradford were here because their countries wanted a part in the city's booming trade. The import and export of goods between Bradford and their country was the main role for these men. Today's Pakistan consulate no longer deals with imports and exports of goods. Their main role is to assist where they can, and are requested, with any problems people of Pakistani descent are having in the city. They are also the point of contact for passports and visas to Pakistan. The large influx of workers from the Indian sub-continent into this city was originally due to the prominence of the textile trade. These people became important members of the Bradford workforce and contributed vastly to the town's prosperity. However, Bradford's textile industry is now virtually non-existent and, ironically, we now import those goods from the Indian sub-continent. As Lord Masham predicted at the opening of Bradford Cartwright Hall Museum and Art Gallery in 1904

I have a very strong impression that the East will overcome the West in the coming years, and that instead of our clothing the East they will want to clothe us.

This speech was greeted with laughter by those present.

REFERENCES

Parker, James – *Illustrated Rambles from Hipperholme to Tong* (includes the opening of the Bradford Exhibition by their Royal Highnesses the Prince and Princess of Wales.)   1904

Local newspaper cuttings, BLSL

Bradford Directories, BSLS

English Census Records, Ancestry.com

Information Resource Centre , US Embassy London

Canrera, Tiffany, Historian Special Projects Division, US Department of State

CHAPTER EIGHT

THE EARLY YEARS OF THE BRADFORD SCHOOL BOARD.

William Forster M.P. has fascinated me for years. I could never understand why he organised the education system of this country the way he did wondering why he kept the divisive system that as an ex school teacher drove me to distraction. So, I decided to use the records at WYAS Bradford to see if I could find answers to my questions.

Bradford has several statues commemorating men associated with the city who have excelled at national level. Near the new shopping centre at the bottom of Bolton Road is the imposing statue of an MP for Bradford who shaped the form of education in this country.

Statue of W E Forster Forster Square Bradford   J C Senior

The 1870 Education Act is universally known as Forster's Education Act after the MP William Forster who steered the **Bill** through Parliament. This act provided a national school system for children from three years of age upwards, led to the establishment of non-religious schools, gave each town the power to run these schools by establishing Education School Boards and tried to standardise, to some extent, the content of lessons taught in schools by providing Her Majesty's Education Inspectors.

W E Forster from "Life of the Right Hon W E Forster" by T Wemyss Reid

Before 1870 five types of schools existed in Bradford each managed by organisations with differing aspirations, their **own** lesson contents and not open to all the population. National Schools were started by the Church of England and funded by the National Society for Promoting Religious Knowledge. Their aim was to provide elementary education in accordance with the teachings of the Church of England. There were sixteen of these schools in the Bradford Directory for 1870.

Original All Saints C of E school buildings   *J C Senior*

British Schools were funded by the British and Foreign Bible Society. These were run on non-sectarian principles and were associated with the non-conformist churches. There were two British Schools in the 1870 Directory run by free churches.

Also recorded are three Roman Catholic Schools, one Primitive Methodist School and four Wesleyan Methodist Schools. These schools attached to churches were not Sunday Schools but provided basic education for the children in the area around the church. A fee had to paid at each school so many children did not attend if there was no spare money at home.

Ragged schools provided free education for destitute children and were mainly found in rapidly expanding industrial cities such as Bradford. They provided elementary education, free food, free clothes and kept the destitute children safe during daylight hours. The first Ragged School was established in London by Dr Barnardo. The 1870 Directory shows two Ragged Schools in Bradford.

Industrial/factory schools were for the oldest children and provided some form of training as well as rudimentary education. Children attending these school were often sent to them from the Bradford Police Court as an alternative to a custodial sentence. The idea was that some form of training for an occupation would stop them leading a life of crime. Some could be residential. The 1870 Directory shows one Industrial/Reformatory School, a School of Industry for Girls, a Model Factory School and a Mill School attached to Mr Wood's mill in Manchester Road. Some boys in danger of leading a criminal life were sent to the training ship Southampton at Hull.

There were seventy-five privately run schools that offered standard subjects and for extra fees, classics and commercial studies. Nine of these schools took boarders. Most were single sex schools. The 1870 Directory gives little information on these schools so it is not possible to say how many of them were Dame Schools.

The question of universal education for all levels of society was a topic that had consumed people's interest for much of the early nineteenth century. Several the middle and upper classes, especially the Anglican Clergy, were not in favour of education for the masses. One Anglican clergyman wrote to the *Bradford Observer*

It is doubtless desirable that the poor should learn to read for they need access to the scriptures but writing and arithmetic will make them dissatisfied with their station in life.

Many middle and upper-class worries were expressed by this comment

Education is prejudicial to their minds and happiness. They will read seditious pamphlets, be insolent to their superiors and it would be expensive for the country.

However, one industrialist wrote

Mass education is vital to our nation's ability to maintain its lead in manufacturing.

In the 1860s the British Government encouraged the building of new schools for the poor by giving 50% of the cost to applicants they deemed suitable. It was felt by Members of Parliament that the extension of the vote to include more male members of the population necessitated a better education system. The Anglican church, worried about the influence of non-conformist churches on these new voters, submitted 2,000 applications for grants.

Religion was the biggest stumbling block to the establishment of a national school system funded by public taxation. On one side were the religious establishments who felt that religion instruction should be an important part of the school syllabus. On the other side were none-religious establishments who felt that religion should be taught as a subject with no indoctrination. The ideal solution would have been for all existing schools to be closed and then taken over by a new national system of Board Schools with no religious affiliations attached to them. This idea would never have been supported by the House of Lords which numbered many clergy amongst their members. It would also have proved to be a very expensive undertaking. So, a compromise had to be reached. This was brokered by William Forster who manage to obtain support for his ideas from both Houses of Parliament. The compromise was

1. All voluntary religious schools, after an assessment by HMIs, were to be allowed to carry on unchanged.

2. School Boards to be established in towns with authority to build and maintain Board Schools where there was a deficiency.

3. Funding for the new boards to be raised from the local rates with building grants available from the central government.

4. Religious teaching in the new schools to be non-denominational.

5. Parents to pay a fee for each child. (Education was not free until 1891 and not fully compulsory until 1899)

Matthew Thompson and John V Godwin from "Historical Notes on the Bradford Corporation" by William Cudworth

The first Bradford School Board met in December 1870. At the beginning it was a non-elected body and fifteen leading citizens such as Matthew Thompson, ex-mayor and brewer, Henry Ripley, dye works owner, and John V Godwin ex-mayor and photographer, volunteered for the new venture. The new government education department had surveyed the established schools in Bradford prior to the act being passed. The Bradford School Board requested a copy of their findings, so they could start their work with information such as

1. The total school population of Bradford i.e. all children of school age living in the town;

2. The present total provision for school children i.e. number of places available in each school;

3. The schools assessed as efficient;

4. The schools assessed as inefficient and therefore should be closed.

Bradford was eager to start the new regime as soon as possible but the new Education Department in London was not yet running efficiently so its reply was delayed. Deciding to collect the information themselves, the Bradford Board members devised a system for collection of data. The town was divided into zones based on the voting districts and two members of the Board were to visit each school in that zone. Each establishment was given a questionnaire to be completed. Mr W Clarke was appointed to visit all these establishments to measure each room, the playground and the facilities. By the end of the exercise the Board hoped to have a comprehensive picture of the provision already available. Another gentleman, known as the persuader, was appointed to visit every house in the borough to discover the ages of all the children and what schools they attended. Armed with this information the Board would be able to pinpoint where new schools needed to be established.

Fifty-two educational establishments run by churches were visited and their initial ratings were as follows

27 were deemed efficient in teaching and accommodation

8 were deemed efficient in teaching but not in accommodation

5 were deemed inefficient in both areas but there was possibility of improvement

12 were deemed so bad that they should be closed.

There were 14,435 pupils between the ages of three and thirteen in these establishments. This does not include the privately-run schools who were referred to as "adventure schools" which catered for 2,809 pupils. Of these schools

1 was deemed efficient in both areas

9 were deemed to be inefficient but improvable

60 "occupied different grades of inefficiency" and needed to close.

The results of the 1870 government survey arrived, and the Bradford School Board compared both results. This was when trouble began as Bradford questioned the government's conclusions. The government survey concluded that there were sufficient places available at the present establishments and therefore no new schools needed to be erected therefore Bradford would not be receiving any grants for building. However, the Bradford Board survey showed that educational provision was not spread evenly over the borough. Some areas of the town had too many spaces available whilst others had a deficiency of places. The Department of Education had not taken into consideration the rising population in some areas. Many new streets, houses and mills had appeared since the government survey had been undertaken and the child population in such places as Otley Road had soared.

Bradford informed the Department of Education that they wished to build new schools in the Otley Road, Barkerend and Manchester Road areas where there were now 1,559 children of school age and school places for only 710 children. Government replied that these children could be educated in schools with places in other areas of the town. Bradford replied that this was impractical and lead to children not attending any school. An impasse seemed to have been reached and would only be broken with drastic action.

Losing patience with London, the Bradford Board decided to force the issue by ordering the construction of four new schools: Barkerend with 500 places, Leeds Road with 500 places Mount Street with 500 places, and Ryan Street with 300 places. When presented with this *fate accompli* the Education Department capitulated and provided a £20,000 grant towards the cost of building the four schools.

Over the next few years Board Schools were erected in all areas of the borough. They followed the same basic specifications and regulations:

1. The school premises was an independent construction under the management of the head master who was answerable only to School Board;

2. Each school provided accommodation for between 300 to 500 pupils;

3. Each school had separate washing places and offices for boys and girls;

4. Each school had three departments each department having a playground attached;

5. Infant Department for children of 3 to 5 years with a large room and a mistress in charge;

6. Girls Department for girls aged 7 + with a schoolroom, a hall and a mistress in charge;

7. Boy's Department for boys 7+ with a schoolroom, a hall and a master in charge;

8. The school could employ one pupil teacher for every 30 pupils in a class;

9. The school could employ an assistant teacher if they employ 2 pupil teachers;

10. Male employees; master £150 per annum, probationer £100 per annum, certificated £80 per annum, assistant £50 per annum;

11. Female employees; mistress £80 per annum, probationer £60 per annum, certificated £50 per annum, assistant £40 per annum;

12. Pupil teacher employee; 1st year £12.10s per annum, 2nd to 5th year £2.10s rise each year, by the age of 16 £17.10s

13. The teacher's role; to mark the register, collect the fees each Monday, manage the stock, implement discipline, ensure religious teaching as per the 1870 Act, instruction to the pupil teachers out of school hours, encourage cleanliness and good manners;

14. Equipment; lesson books etc. were purchased by the school and then sold to the pupils;

15. Terms; the school was open for six hours five days a week for forty-two weeks in the year, there were to be five weeks' holidays and religious days such as Good Friday;

16. Fees:　　　up to 7 years of age　　2d. a week

　　　　　　　7 years to 10 years　　3d. a week

10+ years of age   4d. a week

10+ years part timers   3d. a week

The fees were reduced by ½d. when there were over three children from the same family attending the school. The poorest family could receive free education.

Drawing of a Victorian schoolmistress by Mary Tetlow

Bowling Back Lane School opened in April 1874 with three departments and seven staff members. The Infant Departments records at Bradford Archives show there were 65 children on the roll which meant the mistress in charge could employ two pupil teachers. Attendance at the school varied according to the weather. Snow and rain affected attendance especially as the cobbled streets became slippery and dangerous, so children stayed at home. Unofficial absences were due to exciting events such as Bowling Tide, November

5th, and Barkerend Fair. Illnesses such as measles, whooping cough and scarlet fever were rife in the area and twelve pupils died in the first two years. School inspections from the Department of Education and Bradford School Board occurred twice a year. One HMI wrote

This school is constructed remarkably well. The children are under very good discipline. All the subjects are taught carefully, and the arithmetic deserved special mention.

Cleanliness and good behaviour were a great concern and pupils were reprimanded for being dirty, lying, fighting in the playground and stealing. Not all the parents supported the teachers. One mother arrived at the school to complain about the treatment of her child and swore at the staff. She was asked to vacate the premises and to take her child with her. One mother braved the wrath of the teacher by complaining about the amount of homework her child was given.

When Miss Howarth, the Infant Mistress, left her post in 1876 she wrote in the school log book:

The parents take no interest in the education of their children either in school or at home.

REFERENCES

Bradford School Board Minutes , WYAS Bradford

Bowling Back Lane School Records, WYAS Bradford

Wemyss Reid, T - *Life of the Right Honourable William Edward Forster*   1888

Bradford Corporation – *Education in Bradford since 1870*

1970

Bradford Directories held at the BLSL

CHAPTER NINE

YOUTH OFFENDERS IN LATE VICTORIAN BRADFORD

Whilst researching Bradford Education records held at WYAS Bradford I came across eight letters that intrigued me. Their content recorded correspondence between the Bradford Education Authority and six reformatories for youth offenders. As all the communications included the names of young people I decided to investigate further. This talk was a result of that investigation.

Forms of punishment meted out to young offenders in England began to be questioned by enlightened men and women in the middle of the nineteenth century. At that time, there was no differentiation between the punishments for adults and children. In 1833, a boy of 9 years of age could be sentenced to death for stealing 2d worth of port. At the same time, 15 year-olds could be transported to Australia for seven years for stealing a pair of shoes. But many adults were beginning to question if these forms of punishment were the solution to the problem of rising juvenile crime. Should young people be sentenced along with hardened adult criminals or would it be better to try to change their lives for them?

In 1837, Parkhurst Prison experimented with a reformatory school system for their young inmates. It provided industrial training, education and religious instruction. The experiment lasted until 1864. It was hoped that the young people would, after receiving a basic education in reading, writing and numeracy and learning a trade, no longer turn to a life of crime when reintroduced into society. The experiment was noted by liberal minded politicians and one of them, Lord Houghton (Conservative), in 1846, attempted to push a bill through parliament that would establish a nationwide system of reformatory schools. The bill did not become law, but interest was created all over the country.

After visiting a similar enterprise in Mettley, France, the Philanthropic Society opened a farm colony in Redhill, Surrey, in 1847. The year 1851 saw a conference on youth offending prevention and reformatory schools held in Birmingham. A partial success was hailed in 1854 when the Juvenile Offenders Act was passed. The act saw the expansion of the reformatory system to the whole country. Any convicted juvenile under the age of 16 years of age could be granted a pardon on condition they spent two to three years at a reform school. Before attending the reform school, several days had to be spent in prison, no doubt as a warning to what could happen if they continued to offend in later years. Industrial schools were introduced in 1857 so the younger element did not have to suffer the horror of time spent in prison. Industrial schools took children in danger of committing a crime rather than those who had already been convicted. By 1865, there were 61 reformatory schools, 136 residential industrial schools, 13 day industrial schools and 3 naval training ships. By 1899 the compulsory time in prison was dropped. The 1932 Children and Young Persons Act saw reformatory and industrial schools replaced by Approved Schools and the minimum age for execution raised to 18 years of age. At the same time the age of criminal responsibility was raised from 7 years to 8 years.

Letters from reformatory schools deposited at WYAS Bradford are concerned with the non-payment of fees by the Bradford

Council. Accommodation, education, training etc. at these schools was not free and the home council of the offender was expected to pay the fees. However, this was proving a burden to many councils who argued that the fees should be paid by the sentencing court. Interestingly, the schools are sited all over the country and are for girls as well as boys. Many of the records for male Bradford youth offenders, which always denote the offender's religious denomination, show a large proportion were Roman Catholics. These boys were sent to The Yorkshire Catholic Reformatory School at Market Weighton. Other boys were sent to Castle Howard Reformatory School, the Calder Reformatory Farm at Mirfield, the Reformatory School at Carlisle, and the North Lancashire Reform School at Garstang. Females went to the West Riding Reformatory School for Girls at Doncaster, Arnos Reform School Bristol and the North of England Catholic Girls Reform School Sheffield.

The information in the letters is brief; name of youth, when they entered the establishment and the number of years of the sentence. However, as the offenders were at the reformatories when the 1881 Census was completed, this provided more information i.e. the age of the youth and the place of birth. These were the boys resident at Market Weighton on the 1881 Census

Richard Armstrong	16y	Bradford
Henry Dillon	15y	Bradford
Michael Richard Flynn	15y	Bradford
James Gillespie	13y	Bradford
John Golden	16y	Manchester

John Greenwood	17y	Bradford
John Hall	15y	Leeds
Edward Logan	17y	Bradford
Charles McManus	14y	Bradford
Hubert Morris	16y	Ireland
Thomas Murphy	16y	Bradford
John Purcell	13y	Bradford
John Roach	15y	Bradford
John William Thompson	13y	Bradford.

Market Weighton Catholic Reformatory School for Boys was founded in 1856 at a Roman Catholic teacher training establishment. By 1858 the school was responsible for 200 boys. It was run by the Institute of Charity, a strict religious order who believed in the use of excessive punishment. The boys were taught such trades as tailoring, shoemaking, carpentry, agricultural work in the community farm, stock control, bookbinding and card box making. The establishment was self-sufficient; the farm provided the food consumed by the residents, the shoemakers made and repaired the shoes worn by the boys, the tailors sewed the clothes needed by the residents and the carpenters made and mended furniture. Any surplus products were sold to add to the school finances. Over the years, discipline deteriorated, conditions at the school and the excessive punishments carried out were criticised. In 1906, the Brothers of Christian Schools took over and remained in charge when it became an approved school for boys aged 15 to 17 years of age, in 1933. Scandal struck in the 1990s and it closed in 1994. The records for the school are deposited at the East Yorkshire Archive based at Beverley. The books provide an extensive record of the boys, thus bringing them to life, however they do not cover the period when the boys mentioned in the letters were at the school. There are many boys from Bradford included in the records and two are included here.

James Croan was born in Bradford in 1862. His father, also called James, had died leaving a wife and five surviving children, two boys and three girls. They lived at 76 Longcroft Place, Silsbridge Lane, Bradford. This was the area of the town where many Irish Roman Catholics had settled. It was a slum area with much unemployment and social deprivation. Young James was a factory hand. It was sometimes easier for the young to find employment rather than adults. However, he was also described as

Not under control.

On the 9th of September 1874, he was sentenced at Bradford Police Court with

Placing wood on the railway sleepers in order to upset a train.

The sentence was one month in Armley Prison followed by four years at Market Weighton Reformatory School. James was admitted to the school on the 8th October 1874 at the age of 12 years. The boy had no previous convictions. Unfortunately, he followed no trade whilst he was at the school and was discharged on bail on the 8th October 1878.

The crime for which he was sentenced was undertaken with his friend Frank Mullarkey who also lived in Longcroft Place. James did not have the influence of a father at home and Frank's father seemed to have little influence over his son. Frank, who was also sentenced to a term at Market Weighton, was described as

Running about without parental control.

The incident occurred on the Midland Railway between Manningham and Shipley and the trial was reported in the local newspaper. The prosecutor said

The offence was a most serious one and the result of the said act might have been most fearful to the passengers.

Did the experience turn James away from a life of crime? On the 1881 Census he is a soldier with the Yorkshire Regiment based at Nether Hallam Barracks in Sheffield. However, before long he is absconding, and his life began to deteriorate.

December 1886 at Bradford Borough Court James was sentenced to one calendar month at Armley for assaulting Julia Kirkbride.

July 1887 at Bradford Borough Court James was sentenced to one calendar month at Armley for being disorderly and refusing to quit a public house.

December 1887 at Bradford Borough Court James was sentenced to two calendar months at Armley for assaulting Richard Delaney.

December 1890 James was sentenced at Leeds to eight calendar months in Armley for robbery and personal violence after a previous conviction for felony.

1891 Census in Armley Jail.

1895 At the Leeds Quarter Sessions sentenced to five calendar months at Armley for felony.

October 1897 at Bradford Borough Court sentenced to twelve months in Armley for stealing a case containing medals and coins.

January 1899 at Bradford Quarter Sessions sentenced to eighteen months in Wakefield for stealing a pair of boots.

1901 Census in Armley Jail.

At some point between 1891 and 1901 James married. There are no records of any further crimes committed and he disappears from the 1911 Census.

Michael Larkin was born in Bradford in 1860 to John and Mary Ann who eventually had nine children. John Larkin was a dyer by trade, but he abandoned his family and travelled to America with another woman. The family left behind had no fixed abode. Michael was a factory hand and had already been in trouble with the police having one offence on his record. He was charged on 3rd May 1875 at Bradford Police Court with being:

A rogue and a vagabond

This meant he was a homeless beggar, a state which had been an offence in England since the 1824 Vagrancy Act made it illegal to sleep rough or to beg. Michael's sentence was for two months at Armley followed by four years at Market Weighton. Here he trained as a shoemaker and was released to the care of an elder brother who lived in Leeds Road. There are no records of him reoffending.

The West Riding Prison Records for 1801 to 1914 are viewable on Ancestry. Also, available to view are some records for West Riding Reformatory Schools.

John Roper, born in Bradford in 1864, was sent to the Leeds East Moor Reformatory School on 20th March 1877. This was on Adel Moor and was opened in 1857 for 60 boys. The first intake was employed in building the remaining buildings. As with most reformatory schools the main emphasis was on education closely followed by learning a trade. Boys worked as gardeners growing oats, potatoes and turnips for consumption by the residents or to sell to the public. Some boys worked as tailors and made the establishment's clothes, the shoemakers repaired shoes and the joiners made furniture. Those working on the farm raised cows and pigs and looked after the horses.

Though John had attended Eastbrook school in Bradford, when sentenced, he could not read, write or cypher. His father, Ezekial, was a carter living with his family in the Otley Road area. John had stolen a coat and was sentenced at Bradford Police Court on 21st February 1877 to one month at Armley and four years at Adel. He had a previous conviction where he had been sentenced to a whipping for stealing a hen and a rabbit. When discharged from Adel on bail in 1879, to complete his sentence as an apprentice, his education had greatly improved. John was placed with Mr Stocks, a smack-boat owner in Great Grimsby.

Charles Yeadon, born in Bradford in 1860, was sentenced at Bradford Police Court on 19th December 1876 to one month at a house of correction and four years at a reformatory school for:

Feloniously embezzling 7/- from his master.

Charles was sent to the Calder Valley Farm School. This Reformatory school was opened in 1855 to take 42 boys and was extended in 1859 when 100 were on the register. Like the Philanthropic Society experiment at Redhill in 1849, the school organisation was influenced by the farm in Mettley, France. The boys were organised into family groups.

Being the younger son of a wealthy widow, Charles was not the usual type of youth brought before the court. His mother was living on independent means in Otley Road. Her eldest son became a Methodist lay preacher. His deceased father had been a wool stapler. Charles was well educated and in a steady job as an assistant in an ironmonger's shop. When asked why he stole money from his employer Charles replied he

Wanted money to go to the Music Hall.

On leaving the Farm School Charles emigrated to New Zealand.

The behaviour and crimes committed by these young people are still happening today. A reformatory experience worked as a deterrent for some but not for all. Social deprivation played a part, but it was not the principal reason for turning to crime. When a group of high spirited youngsters get together anything can happen. The punishments meted out in that period may not always appear to fit the crime and it would be many years before a much fairer pattern would appear.

REFERENCES

Boys admitted to the Yorkshire Catholic Reformatory, WYAS Bradford, BB1/1/111/1,6,8,9

Reports on Yorkshire Catholic Reformatory School boys, WYAS Bradford, BB1/1/111/4,5

Bills of maintenance for the West Riding Reformatory School for Girls, WYAS Bradford, BB1/1/111/7,12

Correspondence re Reformatory Schools, WYAS Bradford, BB1/1/111/10

Bills of maintenance for the Yorkshire Catholic Boys Reformatory School, WYAS Bradford, BB1/1/111/13

Concerning boys detained in the Yorkshire Catholic Reformatory School, EYAS Beverley, DDSW/1

Higginbotham, Peter – Children's Homes web site

West Yorkshire Prison Records 1801-1914, Ancestry.com

West Yorkshire Reformatory School Records 1856-1914, Ancestry.com